Studio Joy Works

Studio Joy Works

RICK JOY

Essay by Michael J. Crosbie

———

PRINCETON ARCHITECTURAL PRESS · NEW YORK

Published by
Princeton Architectural Press
A McEvoy Group company
202 Warren Street, Hudson, NY 12534
Visit our website at www.papress.com

© 2018 Princeton Architectural Press
All rights reserved
Printed in China
21 20 19 18 4 3 2 1 First edition

Princeton Architectural Press is a leading publisher in architecture, design,
photography, landscape, and visual culture. We create fine books and stationery
of unsurpassed quality and production values. With more than one thousand
titles published, we find design everywhere and in the most unlikely places.

Editors: Nolan Boomer and Abby Bussel
Design concept: Rick Joy Architects
Typography and design: Paul Wagner
Front cover photograph: Joe Fletcher
Back cover photograph: Jeff Goldberg/Esto

Special thanks to: Janet Behning, Benjamin English, Jan Cigliano Hartman,
Susan Hershberg, Kristen Hewitt, Lia Hunt, Valerie Kamen, Jennifer Lippert,
Sara McKay, Parker Menzimer, Eliana Miller, Nina Pick, Wes Seeley, Rob Shaeffer,
Sara Stemen, Marisa Tesoro, and Joseph Weston of Princeton Architectural Press
—Kevin C. Lippert, publisher

Library of Congress Cataloging-in-Publication Data
Names: Joy, Rick, 1958- author. | Crosbie, Michael J., writer of introduction.
Title: Studio Joy works / Rick Joy ; introduction by Michael J. Crosbie.
Description: New York : Princeton Architectural Press, 2018.
Identifiers: LCCN 2018015335 | ISBN 9781616897550 (hardcover : alk. paper) |
ISBN 9781616896461 (pbk. : alk. paper)
Subjects: LCSH: Joy, Rick, 1958—Themes, motives.
Classification: LCC NA737.J69 A4 2018 | DDC 720.92—dc23
LC record available at https://lccn.loc.gov/2018015335

What We Hold Close | Rick Joy

One place understood helps us understand all places better.

—EUDORA WELTY, *ONE WRITER'S BEGINNINGS*

It has been fifteen years since we made our first monograph, *Rick Joy: Desert Works*, with a moody close-up photograph of "my first house," the rammed-earth Catalina House, on the cover. With that book, we aimed to define our process, collecting into printed form our thoughts on working in a desert context, our use of then-unusual materials, like exposed rammed earth, and our at-once straightforward and deeply emotional approach to the practice of architecture. Now, twenty-five years after forming Rick Joy Architects, I seek to understand place anew.

We have kept our desert home, but beyond that, so much has changed. While my firm began as "local" (to a hundred-mile radius of our studio), it has, over time, extended to sites far away from our strip of land in Tucson, Arizona, to the rolling hills of Vermont, the jungles of Mexico, the campus context of Princeton University, the urbanity of Mexico City, and the island cultures of Turks and Caicos, Ibiza, and Long Island. Yet we have remained dedicated to the same clarity we cultivated so many years ago.

This book marks a moment of transformation: it is called *Studio Joy Works*, highlighting our inclusive, cooperative practice and the works we produce together. When architectural studios grow, the work can often become challenged, diluted into a repeated style; in our case, the referencing of our team as Studio Rick Joy has given us a chance to develop a rigorously clear understanding of what we hold close, of the values that matter to us. It is those values—like being conceptually insightful and giving, cherishing the site's spirit, and honoring the building culture of place—that determine how we do this work.

Our studio is in Tucson, deep in the Sonoran Desert, a wide-ranging landscape that begins in Baja, California, winds its way through northern Mexico and continues north of here. Our compound of seven earthen buildings is in Barrio Viejo on one of the oldest streets in the United States. A wooden door opens into our entry courtyard that is flooded with sunlight; our main work space, a long narrow studio with a glass wall that provides a thin barrier between inside and outside, demarcates this courtyard's edges. A conference room, model shop, and more studio spaces reside in the other buildings that are linked by a series of exterior courtyards and pathways.

The studio campus is one of our earliest works—originally built as artist live-work spaces, the first building phase of which predates the arrival of my first interns. Working in and around these structures deeply influences our process, as we absorb lessons from the architecture and the surrounding environment. The skylight at the end of the main office, the leafy shadows that speckle the white walls outside the studios, the deep shade from the buildings on the paths between, the crunching of the gravel underfoot, the difference between winter and summer light, the times when summer sunsets enter the studio at an angle that requires a couple of us to wear sunglasses at our desks, the months when we work with the doors open and feel the air flow through the studio—these are all experiences that influence the way we create.

A spirit of giving is at the heart of our work as a studio. Our long hours in Tucson and the time we spend together on our project sites reinforce our ability to produce immersive architectural experiences. The cooperative studio extends to the partners we work with—clients, builders, and contractors—everyone who joins our team becomes part of what we do and also changes our makeup. Like a wave, a team swells and crests when gathered together. Through our work we build friendships; as much as our architecture evolved from a ground condition and its sky, our studio operates through a system of

8

interdependence and care. There is an ongoing exchange of vision and dream; it is shaped, massaged, reiterated, refined, and reduced to its essence of an atmosphere in a crafted space. We consider each of our projects an invitation to a way of life as much as an architectural work.

My early buildings conveyed their character through massive earthen walls, through the way structure captures the movement of the day from light to dark back again to light, through spatial feeling and the deeply felt moments of recognition that come with sensing the "thickened atmosphere"—as Steven Holl described it in *Rick Joy: Desert Works*—of our architecture.

This pursuit is not abstract. We have developed modes of working, values that drive our firm, that remind us to be heedful of the constellation of elements that influence design, such as the qualities the site offers, the context, client interests, budget constraints, identity of place, and all the complexities that producing architecture involves.

Being comprehensively observant and sensitive toward the world around us is highly valuable for making architecture that lives well in its surroundings and that is lived in well. Beyond being an object for static photography, a building becomes architecture when graciously enlivened. It is the stage for personal events where daily life and momentary dramas unfold in spaces that we design and build as Architects with a capital *A*. Spaces condition behaviors as much as they are eventually conditioned by their inhabitants. We dwell in architecture and architecture dwells in us.

This view of architecture is deeply humane and unfashionably grounded in patience and perseverance in observing habits, listening to nuances, sensing moods, and reading a place. Unique and intimate experiences involving place, nature, and especially light and darkness perpetually surround us. Whether it's the swirl of yellow flowers beneath the paloverde tree in front of my house, the dark reflections of human shapes on the polished concrete floor at a recent gallery opening in Venice, the smoky coastal morning fog from my youth in Maine, or the few minutes when our immediate atmosphere becomes a deep blue at dusk, there is transcendent power in living in observance of nuance. This nearly constant interaction of seeing and recording has an enormous influence on the work.

Understanding the role of nuanced observation and vivid awareness requires moments of calm and pause during which this sensory attenuation can occur—moments for a receptive, rather than controlling, mind. This helps us to develop and evolve the roots of marvelous building-making and the humanizing virtues that people have craved in their everyday lives throughout much of the course of time. One can gain a sense of place only by taking the time to become intimately immersed in its particular natural characteristics—the characteristics that make it unique at a broad range of scales. Taking the time to get to know the human culture and its rituals, memories, meaning in place, and the wisdom of the established building culture are required before either exactitude or tectonic eloquence can occur.

Of course, this kind of thinking exposes the architect to the risk of getting trapped in the making of formal reassurances. Yet, from my practice, I know that when there is courage to make a bold architectural proposition in a particular place—a proposition that is grounded in a realistic interpretation of human lifestyle, a proposition that can be conceptually thought about first—then all these reflections can be synthesized into the making of an insightful and giving architectural work. These characteristics do not guarantee great architecture, but livable architecture might not happen without them.

As architects, what are the means to enable this process of taking charge of a place's locality without overstating our influence? We do this by working within the interstice and harnessing details: designing an ascent through an immersive stone maze when entering the Woodstock Vermont Farm, or by creating a long driveway to the Amangiri resort in the Utah desert to heighten the sense of discovery. Through constant exploration, we seek the balance between sensually attuned and sovereign inhabitation.

Lately, my studio has been entrusted to expand the notion of place and home to the public realm. Public space deserves the same care in terms of these up-close and personal considerations of attuning as a house—sensitivity to the qualities of grace and calm, experiences that are personable and insinuate connectedness to a place and a community. For example, our design for the new transit hall and market for Princeton University delicately balances both the university's and the township's confidence and pride. Arriving and leaving are embedded in sequences of memorable threshold experiences that derive from an architecture that is grounded in the character of the place and an architectural language that resonates with the local spirit of refinement.

Distinctive to this architectural approach is the emergence of a unique identity of place, without falsifying history—in other words, searching for identity without being identical. We create these unique identities through direct sensory experience and conceptual insight while borrowing from and enhancing the emotional identity inherent to a context. As an example, in my early compacted-earth dwellings, I searched for a unique material presence, an identity of dwelling in the Sonoran Desert that was contemporary yet clearly identifiable as being grounded in the local building culture, and of being from the past, as always having been there. This identity is experiential and is conveyed through the massive character of the walls, through the qualities of light and dark, through spatial movement, and through atmosphere. For our project on

Turks and Caicos, our team trained local craftsmen to produce a vibrant white concrete using almost entirely local materials. The shapes of the house and the feeling of waiting on the dock for the day's catch are the results of the conversation between our architectural translation and the rhythms and patterns of the site.

The places we have been and that remain with us in our memory and imagination commune with the context, culture, and nature of new sites. This connection does not mean that the building and its inhabitants will simply inhabit a place. Rather, it inhabits them, stokes their awareness and soul. It creates lasting sensational depth to live by, getting beyond the surface and into the spirit where place and experience can identify with each other and coexist for a little while.

This kind of harmony and memory exists in the relationships I have had with other architects: through books and by visiting their works, I have communed with Luis Barragán and Sigurd Lewerentz, and listened to Louis Kahn and Sverre Fenn from time to time. I have had the great pleasure of becoming friends with many of the finest architects practicing today around the world, some of them elder mentors.

As I turn sixty later this year, I am taking stock of that milestone and realizing the merits of slowly becoming an elder and more of a mentor myself. Having some of the most switched-on young talents on the planet coexist and cocreate with me for more than a little while is the most meaningful aspect of my career in architecture. It is for this reason that I dedicate this book to all the past, present, and future women and men of Studio Rick Joy.

Marvels of the Day | Michael J. Crosbie

Light is time thinking about itself.

—OCTAVIO PAZ, "SIGHT AND TOUCH"

Rick Joy steers his car onto the shoulder of a residential road in northern Tucson, in the foothills of the Santa Catalina Mountains. We have driven out from his downtown studio in the city's Barrio Viejo, the neighborhood where he has worked for twenty-five years. We're here to visit the Catalina House, Joy's earliest residential project. Out of the car, we walk down a rugged, stone-strewn driveway bordered with desert plants and small holes in the earth—the homes of creatures that emerge mostly at night—and head toward a metal-shrouded garage, beside which a Texas ebony tree presents its brilliantly green leaves, made even more vibrant against the rusty wall of the garage.

As we come to the end of the driveway and into the presence of the house, stillness seems to descend over the spot—as if the architecture itself creates a desert oasis of calm. The discrete edges of the house are difficult to trace, so well does its rammed-earth form hunker down into the site like a desert tortoise. The ramparts are dotted with square windows, whose splayed jambs, sills, and heads magnify and articulate the walls' thicknesses. A gravel walkway leads north to the entry portal, hidden in a pocket of space contained behind an earthen wall to the east. The front door is seven square feet, wide enough to drive earth-moving equipment inside to build the walls and "preserve the native desert around the house," says Joy, who was also the builder of the project.

This rammed-earth structure is made of soil that was trucked in for construction, compressed in forms under great pressure into strong walls that years later show traces of nature's assaults—the wearing away here and there of the rammed-earth-wall surface. The house and its setting are saturated with atmosphere, providing a carefully choreographed, cinematic-like experience of the passing of the day and the coming of the night. The late-morning sun rakes across the house's earthen planes, bringing to mind a line from an Octavio Paz poem.

The Catalina House narrates its life on this land, under the sun and night sky, describing the panoply of light, color, shadow, shade, reflection, texture, pattern, wind, rain, echoes, critters, plants, and dirt. Such stories are found throughout Joy's architecture.

———

Joy grew up in rural Maine, where as a boy he often spent time on his own, exploring the rugged settings of the backwoods and farms. These early experiences were an invitation to engage the natural environment and what he would later understand to be the cultural artifacts of a place. He built forts with what was handy—recycled materials such as old barn siding and spools of baling twine, as well as natural ones like alder saplings—assembling makeshift structures and developing, as he explains it, "an understanding of nature, loving it, being in it."

Time in forests and fields inculcated a sense of resourcefulness, captured in an early twentieth-century verse about legendary Yankee thrift: *Use it up, wear it out, make it do, or do without*. When something broke, Joy learned how to fix it (stranded on a Maine island years back, he successfully patched a hole in his canoe with a piece of torn shirt and pine pitch he collected from a tree). When he took up backpacking, he learned the art of getting by with minimal gear. These skills are evident in his architecture—working with available resources, reckoning out unknowns—particularly his early works, which he physically built and designed, as when he set the heavy roof beams of his family house on his own, using car jacks and leather belts.

Joy's problem-solving approach reminded me of an anecdote I heard years ago from the great Bay Area architect Joseph Esherick, whose artist-uncle, Wharton Esherick, counseled the young designer stuck on trying to figure out a straightforward solution to a perplexing problem. Wharton questioned his nephew: "How would a farmer do it?" Similarly, such writers as James Marston Fitch, Sibyl Moholy-Nagy, and Bernard Rudofsky (all of them modernists) recognized the "native genius" (as Moholy-Nagy termed it) of rural builders. Joy, too, pays close attention to the undercelebrated phenomena of the everyday, the lessons they offer, and how those lessons (particularly with regard to materials, orientation, resource conservation, and form-making) can be translated into contemporary architecture that establishes both a robust sense of place and a setting for often-transcendent human experiences.

A look at Joy's personal photography confirms his habit of recording what others may barely notice in passing: he photographs rainwater running down the plate-glass windows of his studio, the underside of a steel bridge, dust blowing across a desert road, jet contrails in the sky over Portugal, tar patches on an airport tarmac, shadowy reflections in a Venetian concrete floor, puddles of water, his own shadow on a Tucson sidewalk. Joy imbibes the marvels of the day with a profound sensitivity to light, shadow, pattern, reflection, texture, scent, sound, atmosphere, and shifting time that his architecture embodies in all of its sensual dimensions.

———

Joy calls his office a "cooperative practice." He and his colleagues, now some three-dozen strong, display a close working relationship characterized by what he describes as "a shared vision and common aspiration." With staff from Arkansas, Kentucky, Maine, California, Kansas, Texas, and South Carolina, as well as Panama, Mexico, Iran, Sweden, South Africa, Germany, Portugal, Spain, Vietnam, Chile, Singapore, the United Kingdom, Italy, Java, Austria, France, Morocco, Greece, the Netherlands, Australia, Canada, China, Switzerland, and Japan, the studio's global character is reflected in the work, which is increasingly international in its scope.

In the early days of the practice (Joy hung out his shingle in 1993), his design process was more personal, self-directed, internal (designing as well as building). As the complexity and location of the work expanded, Joy developed a working method with his team that preserves his affinity for intuition and narrative. First, extensive and detailed analyses—of the topography, views onto and from the site, prevailing breezes, solar exposure, weather patterns, predominant materials, and existing structures—are completed, which become the touchstones for later design decisions.

In the earliest stages of design, he develops a narrative of its emotive energy, almost a waking dream of what the project might be. At the beginning of a project's design phase, Joy does few if any sketches. Instead, he tries to get his arms around the existential, phenomenological potentials of the location and how the architecture will support them. Joy likens it to the way a director might imagine a film's experiential sequence and begins to visualize and document those experiences with the architecture as the frame. He describes the process as entering a state of being wary of preconceptions, cultivating a sense of openness to the possibilities of the place. He says that this approach discourages the imposition of preconceived ideas by asking over and over, "what if…?" and resulting in the testing of different design alternatives with his team through models and drawings.

For many years before he chose architecture as a career, Joy was a professional musician, and he compares designing to writing songs. According to Joy, someone once asked Tom Waits how he writes a song. "Waits responded that he doesn't write songs, he catches them," notes Joy. "Waits said that you need to make yourself an interesting place for them to land." Studio Rick Joy is just such a place, where architectural concepts can alight and thrive.

———

Studio Rick Joy's exacting details exist in a state of exquisite repose. Take a look at the leather and brass closet-door pulls in the New York Loft, or the rusticated, rubble-wall shower of the Sun Valley House. The gable-end entrance wall of the Woodstock Vermont Farm, where native stone nestles beside graying trim boards, has many lessons to teach, from its snow-and-wind-thwarting entry maze to the composition of its stone end walls. Those walls, as is often the case with Joy's projects, involved a cooperative route to common ground between architect and contractor. To achieve the randomness of the stones' placements, Joy worked closely with the stone masons to devise a detailed set of instructions for sorting pieces by size and color and rules about how to juxtapose them. The poetically variegated walls were achieved by essentially playing a game of "Which stone comes next?" A similar process was used on the slate roof of Bayhouse to produce a highly random texture. A single drawing for a small portion of the roof articulates precise dimensional rules for installing each slate based on size and hue.

At the Tennyson 205 apartment building in Mexico City, there was a design decision to encourage the contractor to use roughly textured boards for the concrete formwork to imprint the wood grain from the boards into the concrete's finished surface and to mill the boards in three different thicknesses with differences of a millimeter. This adds to the variegated quality of the finished wall surface, achieving what Joy describes as "planned imperfection."

Floor plans are carefully regulated to capture experiential events as they unfold throughout the day. Spaces are often contained within rectangles—perhaps a single form (like Joy's studio or Bayhouse) or two forms seemingly meeting in conversation (as in the Napa Tree House). Visitors to Studio Rick Joy's projects find forms that yield to the circumstances of the place, bending around existing flora (as occurs in the Napa project) or volumes that slide past each other and then embrace (as in Le Cabanon, where the utility wing is wrapped protectively around the dining terrace). Two or more rectilinear volumes might crook toward or away from each other in the pursuit of a view at a critical hour, in deference to a landscape (seen in the Sun Valley House), or on a larger scale in the plan of the Amangiri resort, which sensitively captures distinct desert views for each of its thirty-four individual suites by arranging them like a necklace around the site's sandstone Entrada.

Sometimes there is a thickening of plan elements that inhabit a field, which become figural in ways that recall some of Louis Kahn's work. This is visible in the bedroom wing of Bayhouse (where bedroom masses pinwheel off the center gallery), in the entry sequence of the Woodstock Vermont Farm house plan, and in the Adobe Canyon House, whose plan reads as four solid pavilions on a plinth.

Roofs are often recollections and reinventions of lean-to forms—maybe the most common roof type in the world, always ready to shield from sun or wind and to easily shed water or snow. Sometimes, in Joy's work, opposing roofs seesaw or angle ninety degrees from each other—a dialogue among forms that is contrapuntal to the variations on plan configurations. Lean-to roofs sometimes appear inside spaces in obverse. This can be seen in the interior of the Bayhouse, where the main living areas are contained within two tall volumes that suggest the underside of mansard roofs. (However, these volumes are actually carved out of the poché of larger roof shapes as they are expressed on the exterior.) At the top of each volume is a glass belvedere, each with a reverse copper prism that points down into the living space, scattering the orange glow of reflected light.

Perhaps the most spirited example is the ceiling of blackened stainless steel at the Princeton Transit Hall, which evokes the inverted volume of a church nave. (Joy describes the design as a riff on the university's predominantly Collegiate Gothic architecture.) This space has communicated its profound depth. It may be a train station, but the near-spiritual aura of the space makes it seem a perfect place for weddings.

———

A line from the transit hall's sacral atmosphere can be drawn back to the Catalina House, which conveys its own sense of secular sacredness in its roof forms, framed views, and venerated materials. Within its battered earthen walls, the Catalina House contains the silence and solitariness of the Sonoran Desert. Through the thoughtful arrangement of windows, walls, doorways, overhangs, warm woods, and other textured materials draped with light, it welcomes the magical aura of the Southwestern sun reflected off the Santa Catalina Mountains. The house is now more than two decades old, and some of its rammed-earth walls betray traces of their inevitable, slow-motion return to the desert. It will make a graceful ruin.

Michael J. Crosbie, PhD, FAIA, is professor of architecture at the University of Hartford and the editor in chief of the journal *Faith & Form*.

Works

ADOBE CANYON HOUSE

Four rammed-earth corner volumes anchor this intimately scaled house to its southern Arizona site and form a cross-shaped composition of open spaces; the private areas, sculpted within the corner blocks, unfold and link themselves to this carved-out interior. These internal spaces are revealed on each facade, where the fixed glazing to the north and south and silver steel gates to the east and west provide one uninterrupted, reflective, and flush surface. A single silver steel wall cap is visible at the top of the structure and unites the four massive facades.

The house is forty-two feet square in plan, with fourteen-foot-high walls whose texture feels responsive to one's body movement and which produce a vast landscape in contrast with the layout's simplicity. The interior is both refuge and overlook; a concrete floor becomes a patio through the sliding open of large-scale doors. Even larger-scale "paddle-gates" demarcate a transition between the rammed-earth interior walls and the bright desert sun outside. These gates feature large cane bolts at their bases allowing them stay open, no matter what direction the often-strong winds are blowing. At night, the central open axis becomes a clear window, illuminating and drawing visual focus to the human habitat in this wild site.

Evoking the idea of permanence at its first-glance resemblance to an ancient ruin, the house suggests a single block of earth, anchored into the gently sloping landscape. A closer look reveals its textural engagements, as steel meets earth, glazing meets concrete. Its four main exposures frame views of mesquite trees, rolling grassy hills, and Mexico in the distance.

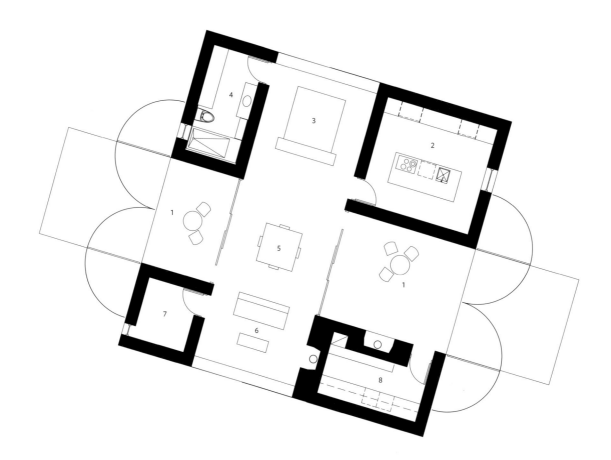

1   PATIO

2   KITCHEN

3   BEDROOM

4   BATHROOM

5   DINING

6   LIVING

7   DEN

8   PANTRY/LAUNDRY

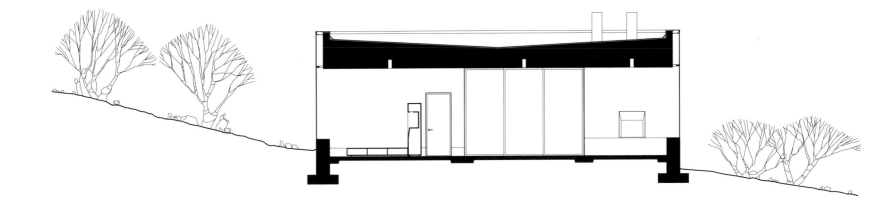

DESERT NOMAD HOUSE

A secluded bowl-like land formation cradles three cubes—the architecture sitting in low-impact equilibrium with the famed Sonoran saguaro cacti. The living room, bedroom, and den each occupy one of the independent structures, requiring travel on footpaths to move between them. These pathways connect visitors to the land and reinforce the house's purposeful seclusion. Our desire to care for the site's fragile ecosystem prompted the elevation of the volumes, which allows water and critters to move freely beneath them and the landscape of eons ago to remain relatively undisturbed.

Each of the three boxes is intentionally oriented toward a singular view of the site's dramatic Tucson-area landscape. The living room looks to the southwest, where, in the early evening, the setting sun highlights a craggy rock hill and draws the eye toward the shadowed foreground at the base of the Santa Catalina Mountains, which are bathed in darkness until the lights of Tucson begin to emerge. The bedroom view follows the rising sun as it illuminates a stunning rock face at the top of the Tucson Mountains to the southwest and crowns the saguaros and ocotillo near the house. In the intimate den, the window frames the nearby rocks and saguaro as if they were a landscape painting.

Steel plate clads each volume, while maple veneer protects the interior walls. The way in which these materials are installed—with articulated panels and exposed fasteners—emphasizes the applied nature of the skin. A ventilated air space behind the skin exhausts heat through natural convection currents. Together, the aesthetic and practical features of the steel skin nod to the logics of nature and remind visitors of the human-made interventions at play.

The interior references the simplicity of the three volumes through its subtle translucent glass partitions and a kitchen island rendered in plate stainless steel. On the roofs, wooden sleeping decks lie flush with the walls, capping each form, and a small carport constructed of steel grating is neatly tucked into a small dip in the entry hill above the house.

0   10 FT.

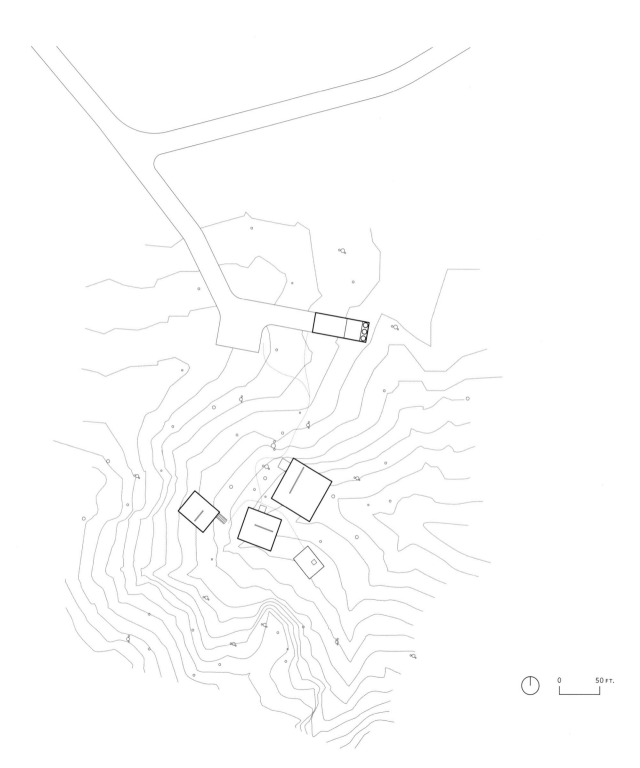

VENTANA CANYON RESIDENCE

Set high on the foothills of the Santa Catalina Mountains and overlooking the vast Tucson Valley, this five-bedroom family vacation house offers a sense of retreat as well as a view from a promontory. A secluded swimming pool and terrace, carved tight to the northern, uphill face of the cliff, allow the house to project out toward the valley as if it were itself a viewing platform. The canyon-like entrance sequence takes visitors along a cascading waterfall and up a flight of concrete stairs to the main living spaces on the second floor. This post-tensioned concrete deck cantilevers thirty feet at the west-end kitchen and twenty feet at the east-end guest house. The lower floor houses the bedrooms.

A heavy-gauge steel skin lends the house a shadowy appearance from a distance, the building's profile flickering in and out of view on the hillside, depending on the light. The lower level, formed in cast-in-place concrete, rests behind steel-plate louvers.

From the second-floor living areas, the valley below is seen through a singular, ninety-four-foot-wide *ventana*, a glazed aperture with cantilevered shades that function like brows. The upper one covers the interior from the sun, and the lower one provides privacy, screening the other houses down below. They create a utopian panorama of the Tucson Valley and distant mountain ranges that are fondly referred to by locals as "sky-islands."

The long, low lines of a swimming pool and footbridge tie the exterior space to the interior's low-slung furnishings and accentuate the long window's presence. The two kitchen islands are arranged to work day and night: for morning seating on the south side, looking north to the side-light crossing on the mountain behind, and for evening seating on the north, looking south to the city lights.

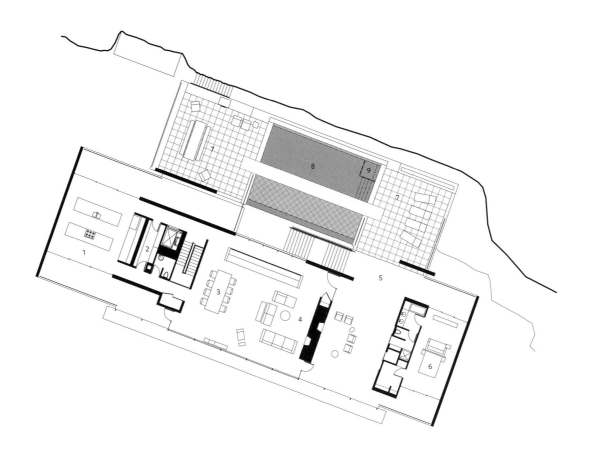

1   KITCHEN
2   PANTRY
3   DINING
4   LIVING
5   BREEZEWAY
6   GUEST SUITE
7   POOL DECK
8   POOL
9   SPA

0   10 FT.

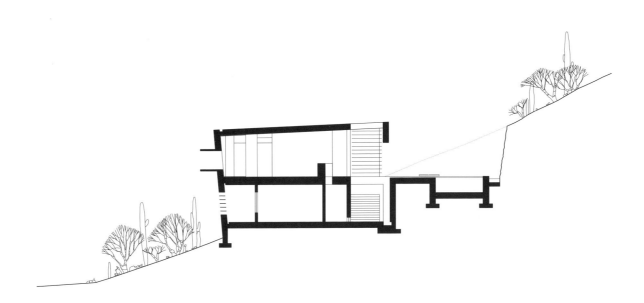

NAPA TREE HOUSE

Tucked into the edge of a forest of ancient oak trees on a remote site high in the hills of Northern California, this off-the-grid house is divided into two wings, which are connected by an entryway and a gallery space. The social wing, which includes the cooking, dining, and living spaces, is flanked by two terraces—one for outdoor dining, the other supporting an elongated swimming pool. This main living space has open views across a ravine to a forest clearing, distant views to the local vineyards, and up-close views in and among the oak trees. The private wing, holding the master bedroom and a single guest chamber, is shielded from view by a tight tuft of trees.

Occupying a hillside site vulnerable to mudslides, the house is built on ninety thirty-foot-deep concrete piers. Exposed concrete walls were formed with three-inch-wide, vertically oriented cedar boards, which imprinted a wood-grain pattern onto both the interior and the exterior surfaces. Outside, the remaining wood fibers have faded to gray from the sun, while inside, they retain a light cedar color that gives the walls a warm glow. The same size and type of boards were used to form the ceilings throughout the house, paralleling the patterns of the concrete walls.

Hybrid skylight-clerestories, in tempered laminated glass and above both the kitchen and the exterior walkway from the carport to the front door, open views through the trees to the sky. In turn, the trees act as filigree lace, filtering dappled light into the house and animating surfaces with a constant reminder of the interrelationship between architecture and nature.

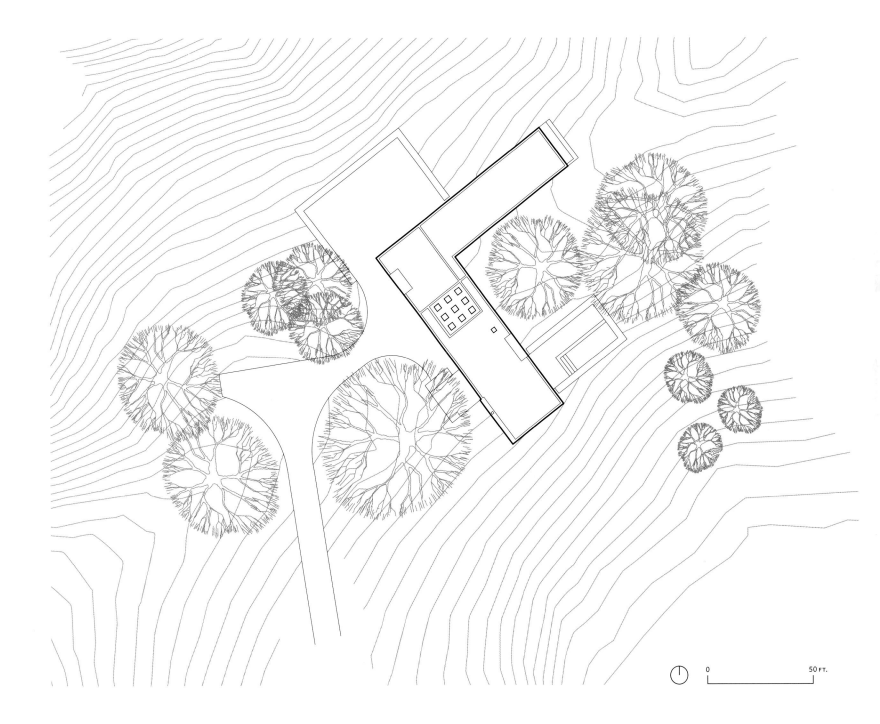

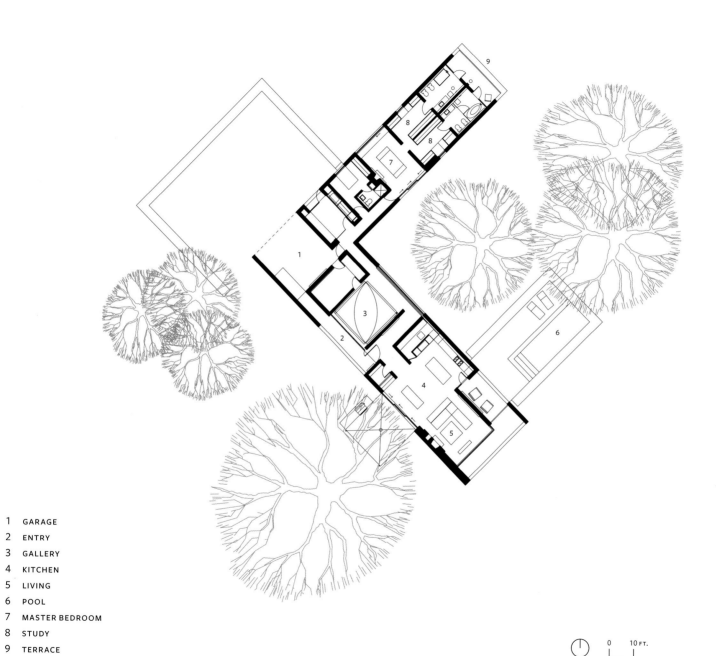

1   GARAGE
2   ENTRY
3   GALLERY
4   KITCHEN
5   LIVING
6   POOL
7   MASTER BEDROOM
8   STUDY
9   TERRACE

0   10 FT.

WOODSTOCK VERMONT FARM

A house, a barn, a farm pond, a deck, fields, forests: a conversation. The house and barn, arranged in relation to the remnants of historic fieldstone walls, the pond, and the road, are simple gable forms representative of an aesthetic familiar to New England farm country.

The house is an elongated, four-bedroom "stone-endah," a regional term for the use of stone as shear walls on the ends of a gabled building. The house's entry sequence, through the east-facing end wall, is an intentionally disorienting stone maze that produces a feeling of compression and then expansion when stepping into the main volume, which leads first through a mudroom and on into the living spaces. Once inside the 150-foot-long, wood-detailed main volume of the house, a nearly continuous series of sliding-glass doors framed with Spanish cedar reveals a dramatic landscape of fields and forests to the north. Structures of steel bents at twelve-foot-on-center operate in concert with the wide sliding doors; the bents are spanned by structural insulated panels and clad with breathable cedar shingles. Large notched openings to the south allow light and shadows to filter into the house through the trees. The interior walls, ceilings, and floors are clad in narrow, perfectly aligned spruce boards.

The two-story barn holds a thirteen-bed bunkhouse upstairs and a farm-equipment garage and half basketball court / multipurpose room downstairs that open up to a large wooden deck extending over the pond. Like the house, the barn is constructed of steel bents, structural insulated panels, and cedar shingles.

My client and friend wanted a "campy chic" vacation home for his family in Vermont. He also, as he told me during our introductory phone call, wanted to bring me back home to New England. We did both.

0   50 FT.

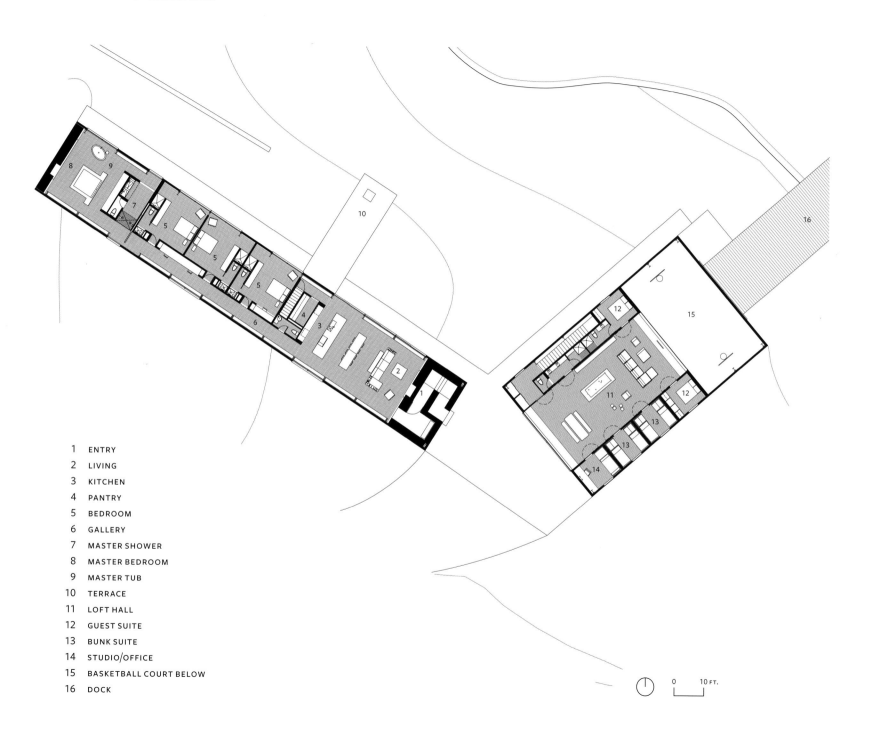

1   ENTRY
2   LIVING
3   KITCHEN
4   PANTRY
5   BEDROOM
6   GALLERY
7   MASTER SHOWER
8   MASTER BEDROOM
9   MASTER TUB
10   TERRACE
11   LOFT HALL
12   GUEST SUITE
13   BUNK SUITE
14   STUDIO/OFFICE
15   BASKETBALL COURT BELOW
16   DOCK

0   10 FT.

AMANGIRI

The thirty-four-room luxury hotel and spa in southern Utah is situated against a low Entrada sandstone formation, as though it were an ancient settlement, allowing guests to experience the raw natural beauty of the surrounding mesas and mesmerizing light shows. The focal point of the resort is its indoor/outdoor living-room lounge and swimming pool, which wraps around a central rock formation, emphasizing the site's essential elements: water, land, and sky. The buildings are designed as thick concrete masses carved by program, movement, and light.

Leading from the main pavilion and pool are two wings that bend and fold against the rock formation. The wing to the east is composed of seventeen suites that are reached via a walled street designed like a slot canyon, replete with the sound of water, the smell of fruit trees, and the refreshing feeling of damp moss. The wing to the south, also with seventeen suites, folds across the desert sands and the undulating rock formations, providing a connection with the surrounding mesas.

The suites are entered through a thick-walled concrete court that opens into a room that affords the guest an exclusive view of the landscape. A raised stone island incorporates a desk, bed, and couch. The bathing and dressing areas are carved out of the thick concrete and lined with green stone and water elements. Outside each suite, a stone plinth terminates with additional lounging benches replete with a private fire pit that captures the essence of desert camping under the stars. Several suites come with private pools as well as elevated sky beds for sleeping under the stars.

The spa is at the end of the south wing. The architecture mirrors the erosion and the silent passage of time that typifies so much of the surrounding rock formations. Wet treatment areas are defined by sculpted organic forms and natural or filtered light, while dry treatment areas are lined with wood and illuminated with colored light.

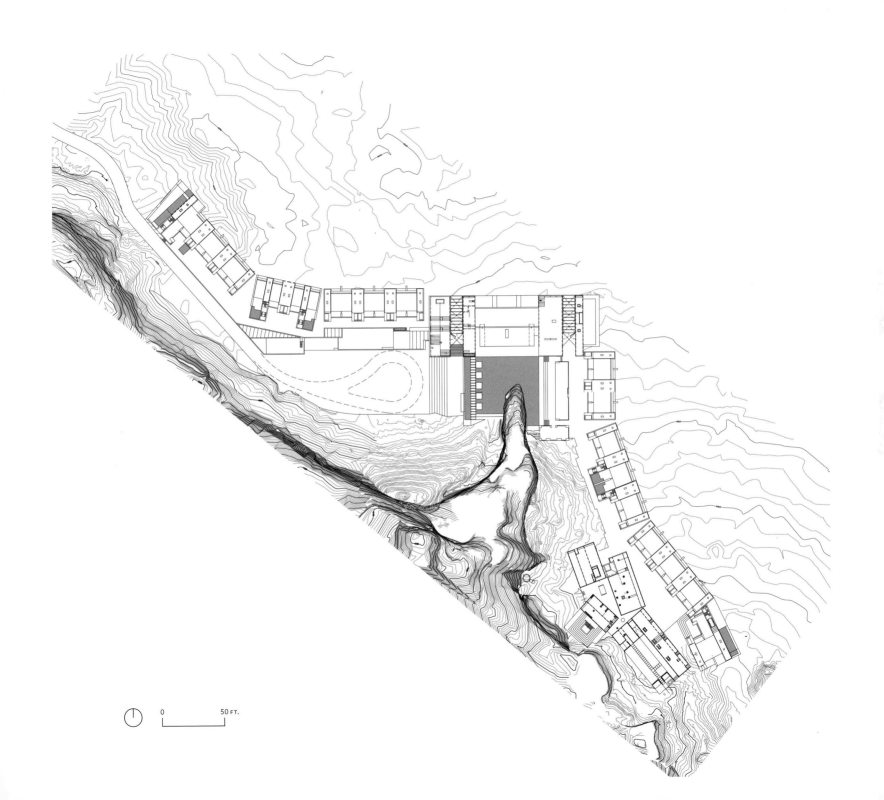

0   50 FT.

LONE MOUNTAIN RANCH HOUSE

Secluded in the expanse of a 27,000-acre Japanese wagyu beef ranch in the high desert of central New Mexico, this six-bedroom family house is a study in opposing relationships between and among functions, walls, orientations, and corners. An indoor-outdoor "living deck"—a wood-floored central space for cooking, dining, and lounging that slips beyond the exterior walls—separates the house's two private zones: one containing the owners' suite and office to the east, the other with spaces for family and guests to the west. A single long hallway provides an asymmetric spine connecting the two.

The interior of the central living space is bright, courtesy of the American Clay wall finish and quarter-sawn white oak flooring and kitchen cabinetry. The island is plate stainless steel, and the fireplace is board-formed concrete using the same white oak that makes up the facing kitchen wall. This space is flanked by window walls with sliding doors that unite the interior and exterior wood decks. The window wall and deck to the north frame the ranch's namesake, Lone Mountain; the window wall and partly covered deck to the south offer sun access and a view of the thunderstorms that often pass by. A lone horse trough and hitching post anchors the southwest corner.

The house's three volumes are united by a single twisted-hip roof whose box-rib panels are made of corrugated galvanized steel. The roof contains a hidden deck for relaxing and sleeping under the stars, with a fire bowl and a telescope for the owner's amateur stargazing. This asymmetrical hip roof is twisted dramatically and ringed by V-shaped gutters, which channel water to two deep cisterns at the opposite low corners of the house, which can be accessed in the event that one of the area's periodic wildfires approach the house. The house's two private volumes are clad in Japanese charred-wood *shou sugi ban* siding, a material known for its fire-resistant qualities.

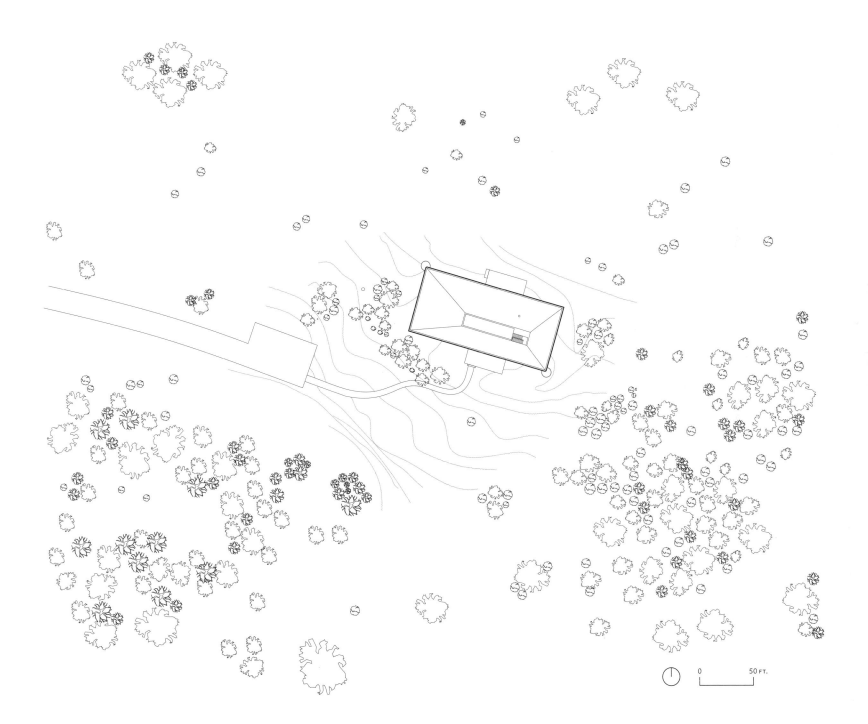

0   50 FT.

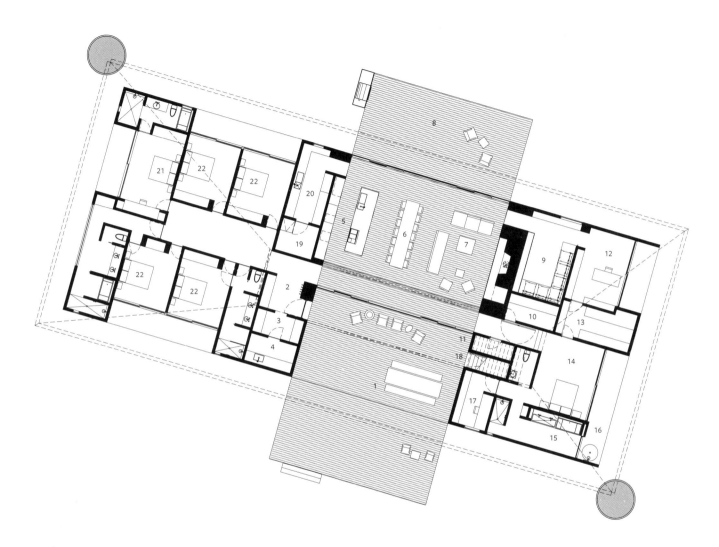

1	ENTRY DECK/PORCH	9	TV ROOM	17	OFFICE
2	ENTRY	10	CLOSET	18	EXTERIOR STAIRCASE
3	MUD ROOM	11	STORAGE	19	MECHANICAL
4	LAUNDRY	12	OFFICE B	20	PANTRY
5	KITCHEN	13	MASTER CLOSET	21	GUEST SUITE
6	DINING	14	MASTER BEDROOM	22	BEDROOM
7	LIVING	15	MASTER BATHROOM		
8	NORTH DECK	16	EXTERIOR SHOWER		

0   10 FT.

SUN VALLEY HOUSE

A quiet family vacation villa is secluded in the arid highlands of Sun Valley, Idaho, just beyond the limits of a designated avalanche chute. The shape of the roof communes with the angles of the adjacent mountains, while each room of the house is oriented to a unique view of the nearby ski slopes and other soft peaks.

The plan features two wings connected by a central axis, which allows for the family's private areas to be protected from the bustle of the social zones by a swath of open space. The guest quarters' position on the lower floor lends increased privacy to visitors and residents alike.

The two shapes surfaced in stone and glass appear from different vantage points to slide together and then pull apart. From the south, the massing appears to be a split-apart gable: two coated-steel forms meet at a central stone vertical structure. The large entry pivot door is accessed from a covered veranda.

The stone masses emerge vertically in the living-room fireplace and twist ninety degrees in the kitchen/dining fireplace. Deep recesses allow for a variety of privately scaled moments. The partially covered northern terrace also has a fireplace and a stair leading up to a hidden roof terrace, which offers a 360-degree view that can be enjoyed from chaise lounges, as well as the opportunity to sleep under the stars in the warm summer months.

Local small-rubble stone, rendered monumental with flush mortar, also defines the fireplaces and complements the lightweight-frame, metal-clad forms. However different in texture, these stone and metal materials softly blend with the sage, gray, and blue of the natural landscape.

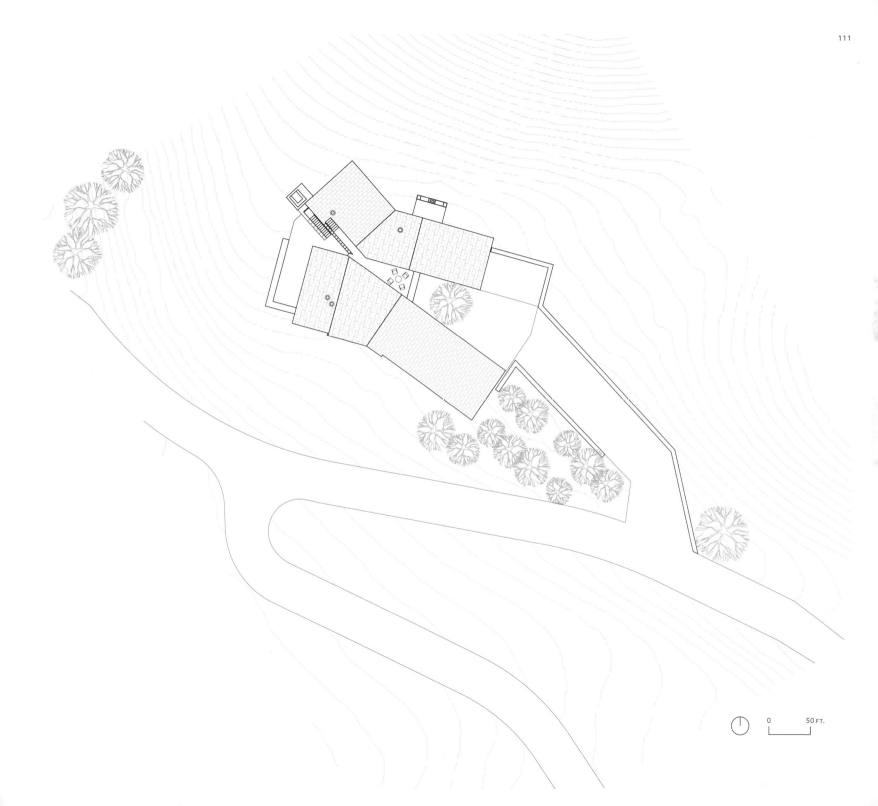

0   50 FT.

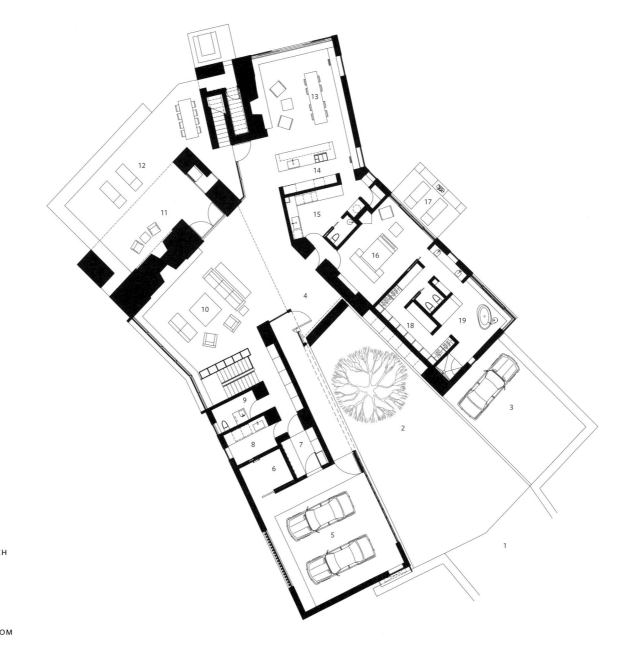

1   DRIVEWAY
2   ENTRY COURT
3   PARKING
4   ENTRY
5   GARAGE
6   STORAGE
7   SKI GALLERY
8   LAUNDRY
9   POWDER ROOM
10   LIVING ROOM
11   EXTERIOR PORCH
12   TERRACE
13   DINING
14   KITCHEN
15   PANTRY
16   MASTER BEDROOM
17   MASTER TERRACE
18   MASTER DRESSING
19   MASTER BATH

0   10 FT

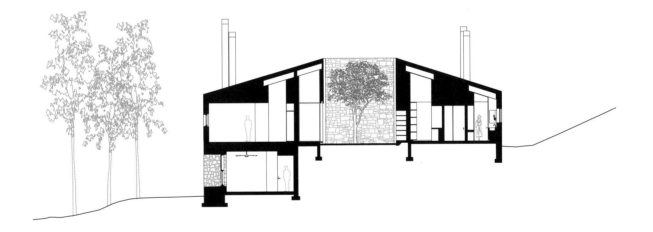

NEW YORK LOFT

Designed as a workplace city retreat for a repeat client-turned-close-friend, who conducts business in nearly every major time zone, the open loft is a thousand-square-foot space divided by the use of light and furnishings into distinct areas: cooking, sleeping, eating, and gathering. Planks of Dinesen Douglas fir flooring, each more than seventeen inches wide, line the floor and continue up the walls to become cabinetry, with tiny leather-strap pulls. Inside the cabinetry is cost-effective, freestanding open shelving.

The centerpiece of the apartment is the sleeping zone, defined spatially by a dramatic bed detailed with thick, gray-and-black puddled curtains that, when drawn, provide blackout opacity from inside the sleeping area and, when pushed to their corners, create a four-poster bed. This formal and functional flexibility both demarcates space and provides for the client's dynamic sleeping schedule. By blacking out only the bed, the one-room loft remains usable by others even when the client is asleep.

A single narrow table is made of the same Dinesen Douglas fir. Because of the inaccessible ceiling structure, the table is lit by carbon-fiber garden table lights. The chairs are made from compressed used denim. This table and light mark the working/dining area and the transition zone between public and private, which allows the more public living room to be illuminated by its full northern exposure, dimmed only by lacy white scrims between the secluded interiors and the busy streets of Chelsea outside. The view to the north frames vignettes of the life of a small church across the street.

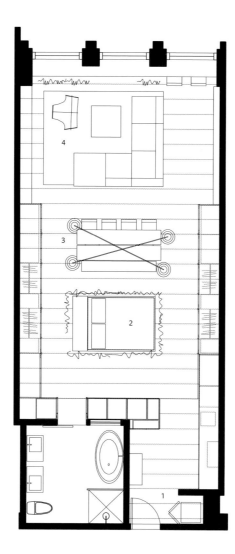

1   ENTRY

2   ENCLOSED BED

3   DINING

4   LIVING

0   10 FT.

LE CABANON

On an inland waterway close to the southwest coast of the Providenciales island on the Turks and Caicos archipelago, we created a three-bedroom family retreat for good friends. The compound is designed to appear as an extension of the coastline along this shallow inlet of white sand and bright turquoise water and to read as nothing more than a high landscape wall from the adjacent road. Porous iron shore rock and rich native vegetation surround the house, and the exposed cast-in-place white concrete walls contrast with its warm mahogany doors, windows, and ceilings.

A large terrace connects the discrete components of the house. To the west, an elongated bar-shaped volume holds the private living areas and protects the compound from the noise and traffic of the street. To the east, a living-dining-kitchen pavilion opens to the water and ocean views.

The open-air pavilion utilizes cross ventilation instead of air conditioning. An operable triangular window at the leeward tip of the pavilion's asymmetric, single-hip roof helps maximize airflow. Similar resource-efficient strategies are evident in the water-harvesting system—a large cistern beneath the main terrace—and in the solar panels that sit below the parapet on the flat portions of the roof.

The white concrete walls—constructed by local builders trained by our office to produce the kind of sheer surface the project required—were built using locally sourced sand and aggregate to minimize the amount of imported building materials used for this island project while keeping the interior spaces cool during the hot and humid days.

Fishermen stop by from time to time at one of the small Ipé docks to offer their day's bounty.

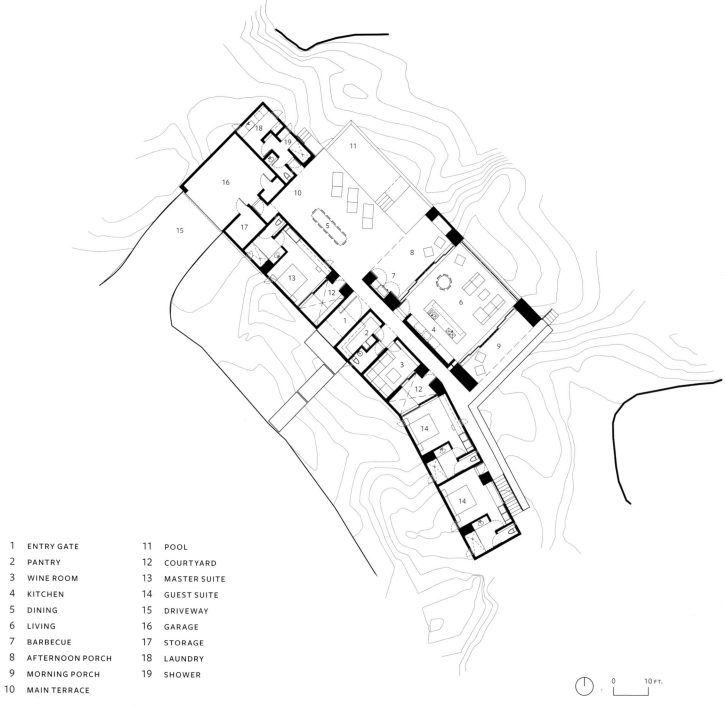

1   ENTRY GATE
2   PANTRY
3   WINE ROOM
4   KITCHEN
5   DINING
6   LIVING
7   BARBECUE
8   AFTERNOON PORCH
9   MORNING PORCH
10 MAIN TERRACE
11 POOL
12 COURTYARD
13 MASTER SUITE
14 GUEST SUITE
15 DRIVEWAY
16 GARAGE
17 STORAGE
18 LAUNDRY
19 SHOWER

0   10 FT.

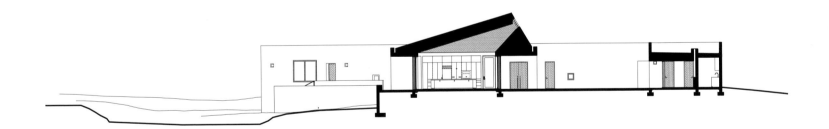

TENNYSON 205

This five-story apartment building is located along a quiet street in Polanco, a thriving neighborhood in the heart of Mexico City. Surrounded by buildings on three sides, Tennyson 205 is an infill project that opens to the city only via its west facade. Three light wells—each vegetated using a variety of planters, boxes, and hanging vines to add greenery and softness to the exposed concrete structure—ensure that daylight reaches the lower levels of the block.

At street level, a blackened-steel gate, detailed with brass inserts, leads into the spatial rhythm of the courtyard, which is illuminated from the light wells above. A narrow staircase leads to the second story, its solid steel-plate structure enlivened by a winding, brushed-brass handrail.

Each of the two apartments spans two floors. The lower apartment can be accessed on the second floor through a double-height, lushly planted outdoor porch, which connects the inner access of the building with the street. From its main living-room terrace, the upper penthouse provides stunning views of the nearby Parroquia de San Agustín and the dense Polanco skyline.

A limited palette of materials, informed by local building traditions, gives the building the appearance of a carved urban sculpture. Cast-in-place concrete, formed with rough-sawn boards, serves as both earthquake-resistant structure and surface finish, giving texture to the walls when they are grazed by light. The coffered ceiling structure is of mostly smooth, form-finished concrete. The floors are covered in hardwood boards, while a number of the rooms feature suspended wood ceilings. Local travertine slabs are used for the vanities and bathroom walls. Slim-profiled, custom-steel casement windows, inspired by a traditional square-frame grid, create generous openings to the outdoors and the city beyond.

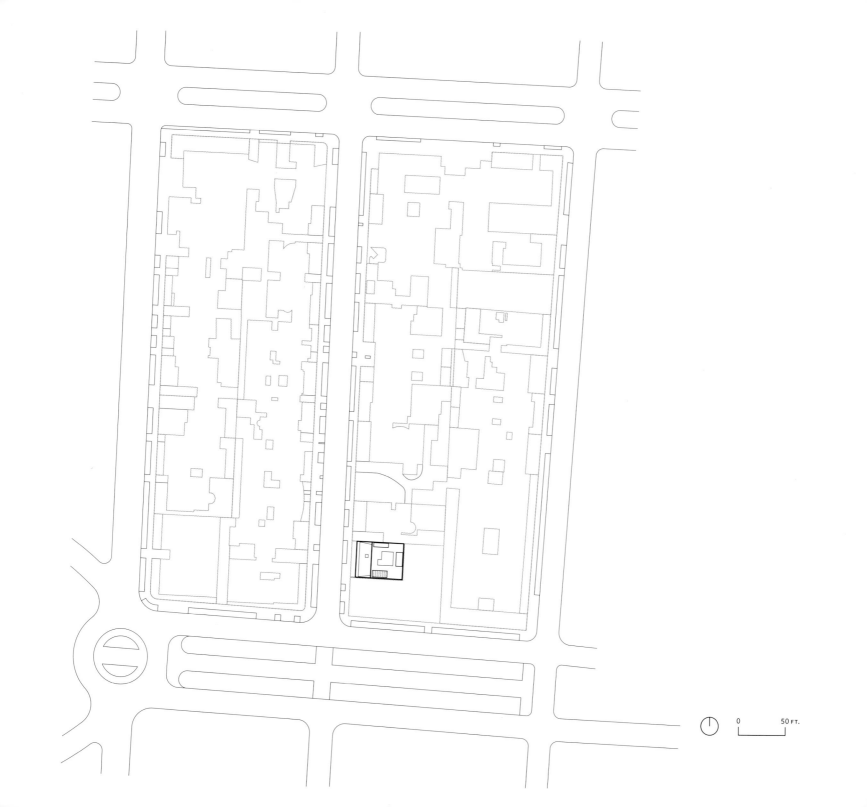

0   50 FT.

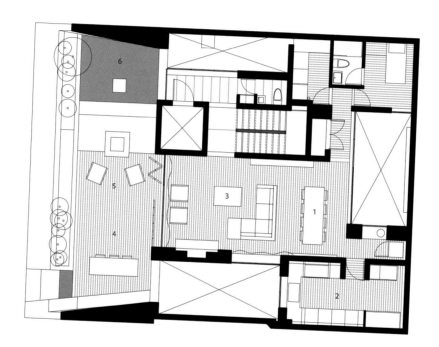

1   DINING

2   KITCHEN

3   LIVING

4   PATIO

5   FIREPLACE

6   REFLECTING POOL

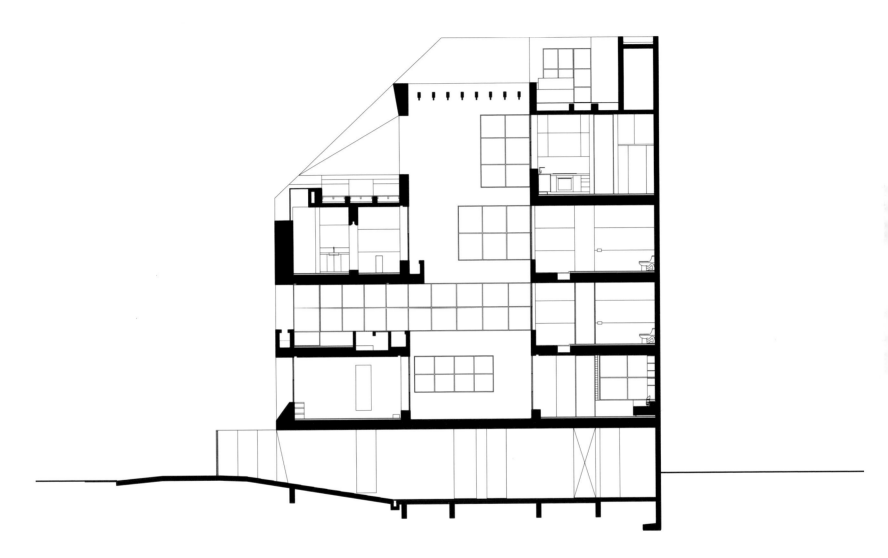

BAYHOUSE

Facing southeast toward the bay, this weekend house sits exposed on a grassy field along a beach, with views across the water to islands and other protected wilderness areas.

In its materials, the house takes some cues from local building history. A steep slate roof sheds rain and snow in the same way as the seventeenth-century wood-shingled houses of the area, but the white-painted, clapboard wood siding typical of seaside homes in the area is reinterpreted as stacked white granite with hand-carved sloped windowsills and thresholds. A car porch lined with Spanish cedar and carved into the stone facade provides shelter from the weather and creates a robust entryway, while a long circular driveway allows the owners to drive in and out in one direction.

Exposed, weighty Douglas fir timbers frame the ceilings, extending into two belvederes—one over the living room, the other over the kitchen/dining area. Sunlight floods in from above, lending a soft warmth to the hand-brushed beams and flamed stone of the interior. The open living, dining, and kitchen spaces are bisected by a massive fireplace that acts as the house's center.

The house's main space is bookended by bedroom suites to the northeast and a screened porch to the southwest. Between the bedrooms, a close spatial arrangement of public zones creates an intimate gallery for displaying photography, while the screened porch offers a view of the public dock and marina.

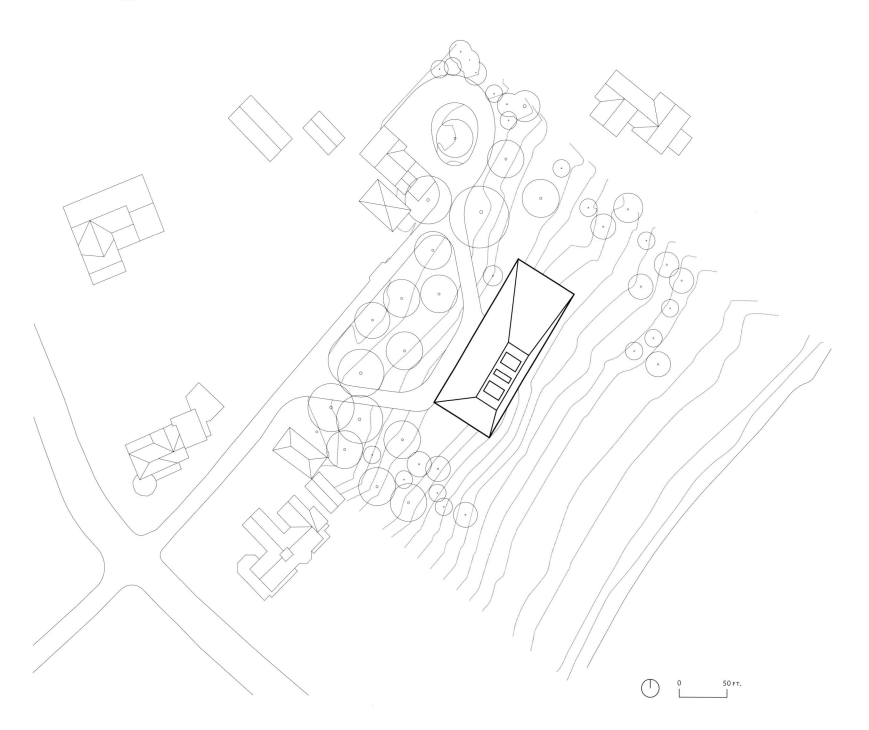

0   50 FT.

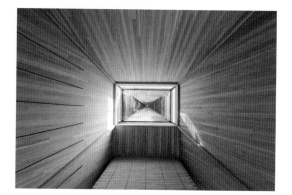

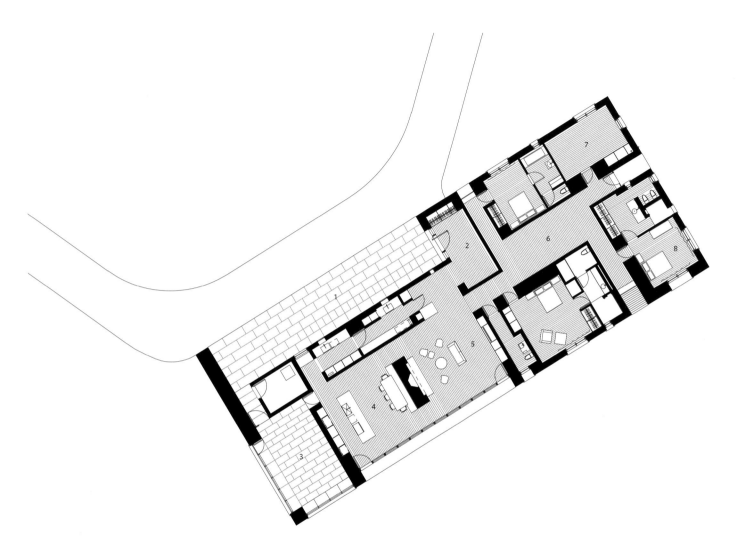

1   COVERED CAR PORCH

2   ENTRY

3   SCREENED-IN PORCH

4   KITCHEN

5   LIVING

6   GALLERY

7   EXERCISE

8   MASTER BEDROOM

0   10 FT.

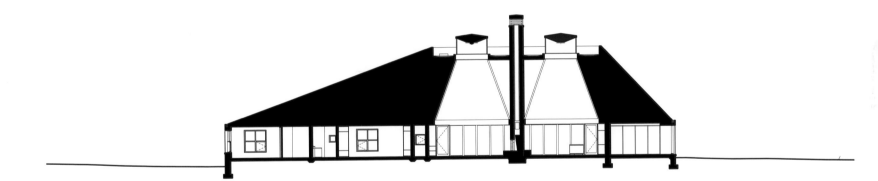

PRINCETON TRANSIT HALL AND MARKET

For Princeton University, we created a new transit hall, restaurant, and market store, oriented around a large plaza six hundred feet south of the existing station. To the south, the blackened stainless steel market with a green roof elevates the aesthetic of the generous bluestone transit plaza, which is in turn flanked on its north side by the transit hall. An additional piazza resides on the north. A two-hundred-and-fifty-foot-long blackened stainless steel canopy and a bike-storage facility across the tracks, as well as the restoration, historic preservation, and addition to the existing station complete the project. This new gateway complex greets visitors in a way that heightens their expectations and celebrates the life and activity of this thriving place.

The transit hall's form is defined by stacked, sand-colored precast-concrete pillars of various widths and heights that gradually increase toward its highly visible northwest corner. A row of columns, separated by benches, are touched by sunlight, visible from arriving trains in the morning and from departing trains in the early evening. The precast-concrete benches on the south face of the station receive full sun, while the opposite-facing benches inside allow waiting passengers to sit with the sun warming their backs. The northern columns, the widest columns, act as barriers blocking the cold northern exposure. The hall is an iconic presence on the site, in spatial camaraderie with the vertically oriented Collegiate Gothic architecture that has long distinguished the Princeton University campus.

The intimate interior black walnut benches, designed with Mira Nakashima and the team at George Nakashima Woodworker, complement the building's monumental scale. These benches provide moments of repose and stillness while also creating a rich tactile connection for the visitor. This material richness extends to the windows, which are framed with three-inch-thick white oak. In combination with the custom pendant downlights in the interior, the space emits a warm and welcoming glow.

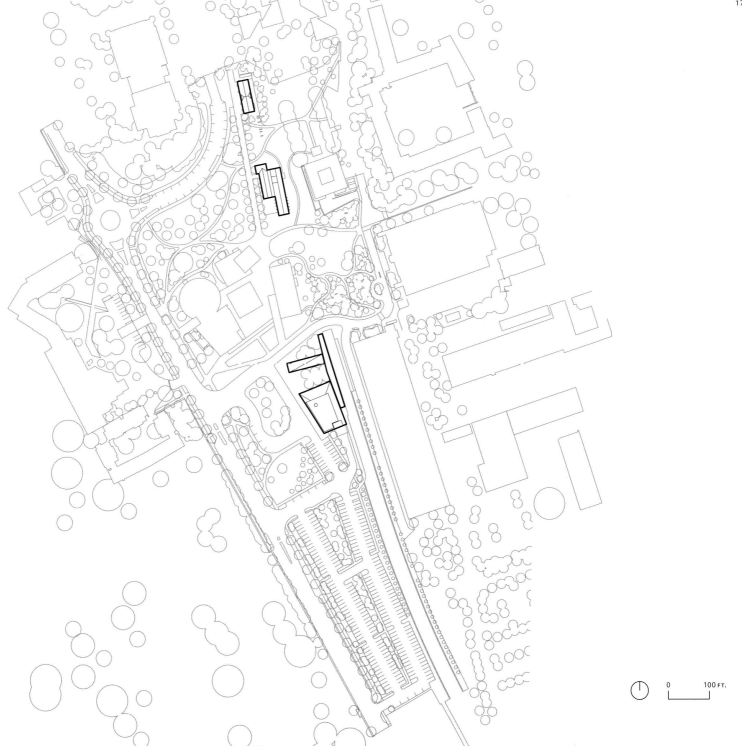

0   100 FT.

1 TRANSIT PLAZA
2 TRANSIT HALL
3 TRAIN PLATFORM
4 COVERED BIKE PARKING
5 LOADING
6 MARKET
7 STORE ENTRY
8 NJT CREW QUARTERS

0   10 FT.

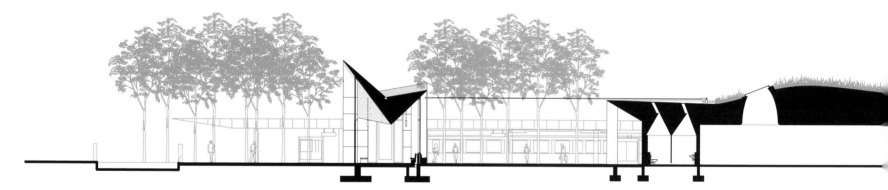

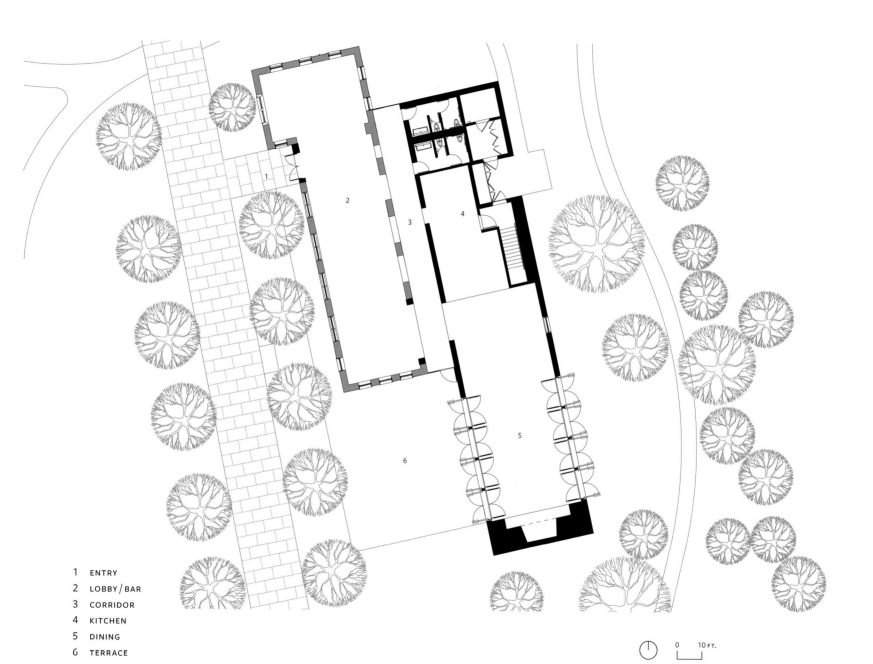

1   ENTRY
2   LOBBY / BAR
3   CORRIDOR
4   KITCHEN
5   DINING
6   TERRACE

0   10 FT.

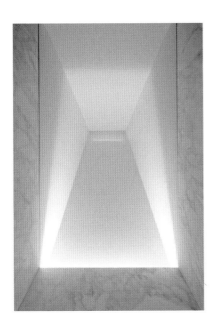

Appendix

Acknowledgments

As we release this book into the world as an insight into how we do things from within Studio Rick Joy, I want to thank everyone who has walked, talked, and paved this road of many forks with me—to all those who have contributed with their care and hearts while growing personally and helping me to transform Studio Rick Joy's work and creative culture into the most rewarding life we could have imagined.

Thanks to Abby Bussel and Nolan Boomer, our editors, and Paul Wagner, our graphic designer, for their continued stewardship of our ideas and patience with our controlling minds in this endeavor. Thank you to Michael J. Crosbie for writing "Marvels of the Day" while rekindling our friendship, which dates back to 1993, when you wrote the first article in an architecture magazine about our studio's work.

Philipp Neher, Claudia Kappl, Matt Luck, and Eva Hagberg Fisher provided valuable counsel on the shape and texture of the voice of this book. Natalia Hayes, Gustavo Ramirez, Trevor Cordivari, and Colby Ritter offered further refinement, having taken the time from their architectural work to craft, consider, and collect all the materials.

We have been very fortunate to have the opportunity to work with some amazing photographers whose images are found in this book: Jeff Goldberg of Esto from New York, Joe Fletcher from Oakland, Bill Timmerman from Phoenix, Undine Prohl from Santa Monica, Jeremy Bitterman from Portland, Jean-Luc Laloux from Bioul, and Peter Ogilvie from Santa Fe.

While I built my first house with my own hands, the work we have done for twenty-five years could not have happened without our builders, consultants, fabricators, and others. I am grateful to all of our construction partners for working so carefully to translate our focused thoughts into built form. None of this could have happened without our clients, who have walked roads of bravery, contemplation, persistence, and dedication with us. We are forever grateful to each of them.

Studio Rick Joy has been graced by the hands and minds of some quite remarkable women and men who have come in early, stayed late, and contributed their sense of humor, dedication, and remarkable talents to the creation of the work I am so proud to have done with them. I am so proud of the strength and length of the relationships that have begun in our strip of land and endured with me. Thank you all.

I also want to thank my sons Ethan and Eli, the Joy Boys, and their mother-spirit, Jean, for all their support and tolerance over the years.

For the last ten years, the work, the studio, this book, and my growth have been greatly enriched by my wife, friend, and closest confidant Claudia Kappl. Five years ago we launched CLL Concept Lighting Lab LLC together, a lighting design company that provides invaluable contributions to all of our projects and others, but more important, she brings to our lives a feeling of constant collaboration and partnership. She is my most trusted sounding board, and I am in awe of her dedication, talent, and commitment to our shared creative life.

Biography

Rick Joy is the founder of Rick Joy Architects, an award-winning architecture, interiors, and planning firm based in Tucson, Arizona.

Rick Joy Architects (RJA), also known as Studio Rick Joy, has been recognized for its sensitive and thoughtful approach to site, observation, process, landscape, and building. The studio's work has encompassed intimate single-family homes and large-scale master plans, and has included residential commissions in Miami, New York City, San Francisco, Tucson, Costa Rica, and Turks and Caicos, as well as lifestyle-based projects in Nayarit, Mexico City, and Austin. Recently, the studio brought new life to Princeton University with the Princeton Transit Hall and Market and is currently finishing a One & Only Resort, for which the studio is responsible for everything from the master plan to the cutlery.

The studio's work has been widely published, appearing in *Cereal, Architectural Record, A+U, GA Houses, Architectural Digest, Travel + Leisure,* the *New York Times,* and *Vogue.* Joy has been a visiting professor at Harvard University, Rice University, Massachusetts Institute of Technology, and the University of Arizona. He is the founder of the Immersion Vermont Master Class, a weeklong program for midcareer architects, and the cofounder, with Claudia Kappl, of Concept Lighting Lab, which provides lighting for all RJA projects as well as for independent commissions.

Joy has lectured and exhibited around the world and is professionally affiliated with the College of Fellows of the American Institute of Architects; the American Academy of Arts and Letters; Civitas Sonoran; the Museum of Contemporary Art, Tucson advisory board; the Scottsdale Museum of Contemporary Art advisory board; CRATerre; and the Ghost Lab advisory board. He is the recipient of the 2002 American Academy of Arts and Letters Award in Architecture and the 2004 National Design Award from the Cooper Hewitt, Smithsonian Design Museum, and he is a fellow of the Royal Institute of British Architects.

Joy was born and raised in Maine.

Chronology

2017

AIA Arizona State Conference "Design Matters,"
Keynote Interview

Visiting Professor and Walton Critic at Catholic
University

Tutor/Organizer of Immersion Vermont Master Class

Film: *Welcome Home*, National Building Museum,
2012–2017

Lectures: University of North Carolina; AIA Billings;
Rensselaer Polytechnic Institute School of
Architecture; Masters of a Generation; and
Dalhousie University

2016

International Fellow of the Royal Institute of British
Architects

Inducted into the National Academy of Design

Tutor/Organizer of Immersion Vermont Master Class

Jury: Jeff Harnar Award for Contemporary Architecture

Film: *Welcome Home*, National Building Museum,
2012–2017

Lectures: AIA Colorado; AIA New Jersey; AIA Arizona/
University of Arizona; and New School of
Architecture

2015

International Fellow of the American Institute of
Architects, College of Fellows

Served as AIA Santa Fe Design Awards Chair

Tutor/Organizer of Immersion Vermont Master Class

Visiting John Portman Chair at Harvard Graduate
School of Design

Somerville Lecturer at University of Calgary

Film: *Welcome Home*, National Building Museum,
2012–2017

Lectures: University of Calgary and the Architectural
League of New York

2014

Architectural Record Houses Award for Sun Valley House

Tutor/Organizer of Immersion Vermont Master Class

Film: *Welcome Home*, National Building Museum,
2012–2017

Lectures: 361 Degrees Conference; University of
Washington; and Architectural Record Innovation
Conference

2013

Jeff Harnar Award for Contemporary Architecture in
New Mexico for Lone Mountain Ranch House

Tutor/Organizer of Immersion Vermont Master Class

Film: *Welcome Home*, National Building Museum,
2012–2017

Lectures: Florida International University; Museum of
Contemporary Art, Tucson; AIA San Antonio;
University of Colorado; Rural Studio; Montana State
University; AIA Arkansas Convention; University of
Las Vegas; and Clemson School of Architecture

2012

Local Genius Award from Museum of Contemporary
Art, Tucson

Adjunct Professor at University of Arizona

Married Claudia Kappl

Alumnus of the Year from University of Arizona

Taught Blue Mountain Master Class at Architecture
Foundation Australia

Visiting Professor of Architecture at Harvard University
Graduate School of Design

Film: *Welcome Home*, National Building Museum,
2012–2017

Exhibitions: *Venice Biennale* and *5 North American
Architects* at GA Gallery

Lectures: Sustaining Identity III Symposium Keynote;
Friends of Futuna Lecture Series; and New Castle
University

Film screening and interview: Checkerboard Film
Conversations, Venice Biennale with Steven Holl.

2011

Adjunct Professor at University of Arizona

Exhibition: *From Earth and Clay in Tlemcen, Algeria*

Lectures: Reinvention Symposium Keynote; Washington University; and Ghost International Architecture Conference Keynote

2010

Architectural Record Houses Award for Woodstock Vermont Farm

Film screening and interview: Checkerboard Film Conversations

Exhibition: *Lone Mountain Ranch House* at GA Gallery

Lectures: University of Puerto Rico; Australian Architecture Association; North American Anthology Conference; Ghost Conference; and Arizona State University

2009

Architectural Record Houses Award for Ventana Canyon House

Mario Pani Award from Universidad de Anahuac

Symposium and Keynote in Bogotá, Colombia

Latitudes Symposium Keynote

Visiting Professor of Architecture at Harvard Graduate School of Design

Film: *Rick Joy: Interludes*, produced by Checkerboard Film Foundation

Exhibitions: *Casa Linda and Marfa House* at GA Gallery and an exhibition at Cooper Hewitt, Smithsonian Design Museum

Jury of Texas Society of Architects Awards

Mundaneum Symposium Keynote

Design Conference Keynote

Alvar Aalto Symposium Guest in Jyvaskyla, Finland

Architectural Biennale Keynote in Lima, Peru

Lectures: University of Dalhousie; Mississippi State University; and Tecnologico de Monterrey Mexico

2008

American Architecture Award for AvraVerde project with exhibitions in the United States, Italy, and Greece

Exhibitions: *Desert Pavilions and Woodstock Farm* at GA Gallery and at Zaragoza Exhibition, ZK-Architectures for a Sustainable Planet

One-month excursion throughout Mali and Dogon Villages

Lectures: University of Arizona; Expo on Water and Sustainable Development; and National University of Singapore

2007

American Architecture Award for AvraVerde project with exhibitions in the United States, Italy, and Greece

Lectures: Desert Tourism Conference at Harvard Graduate School of Design; and Professional Lighting Design Association Conference

2006

Visiting Professor at Massachusetts Institute of Technology

Exhibitions: *Casa Marbella and Desert Nomad House* at GA Gallery

Lectures: Keynote Cartegena Summer Conference; AIA Baton Rouge; Museum of Art, Oslo; International Conference Keynote in Mexico, DF; Architectural Association of Ireland; and Royal Architectural Institute of Canada

2005

Architectural Record Houses Award for Desert Nomad House

Lectures: École d'Architecture de Paris-Belleville; École d'Architecture de Grenoble; CRAterre; Hospitality Conference Keynote; Harvard Graduate School of Design; International Conference Keynote in Santiago, Chile; Auckland University; Danish Institute of Architects; Museum of Art in Palm Springs, California; University of Arizona; and Museum of Contemporary Art, Tucson

2004

National Design Award from Cooper Hewitt,
Smithsonian Design Museum
Keynote: International Conference Bienal de
Arquitectura in Santiago, Chile
Visiting Professor at the Graduate School of Design
at Harvard University
Lectures: University of Colorado; Iowa State University;
North Carolina State University; Kansas State
University; Denver Museum of Contemporary Art;
and National Building Museum

2003

Visiting Cullinan Chair and Professor at Rice University
Lectures: Alvar Aalto Symposium Keynote in Jyvaskyla,
Finland; Cooper Hewitt, Smithsonian Design
Museum; AIA Baltimore; Graham Foundation;
Dalhousie University Halifax; Yale University; Rice
University; Pratt Institute; and Santiago de
Compostella

2002

Juror of *Architectural Review* AR+D Awards
Visiting Critic at Rice University, Arizona State University,
and Washington University
American Academy of Arts and Letters Award, Academy
Award in Architecture
Exhibitions: *Ten Shades of Green* shown at the City
College of New York, Washington University,

University of Arizona, and American Academy
of Arts and Letters
Lyceum Fellowship Chairman
Participant in Harvard University's Summer Executive
Conference "Practicing Out-There"
Jury of Seattle AIA Design Awards
Published *Rick Joy: Desert Works* (Princeton
Architectural Press / Graham Foundation)
Participated in "Architecture for All" conference
National Design Award Finalist in the Smithsonian
Institute's White House Ceremony
Lectures: University of Idaho; Alaska Design Forum;
AIA Baton Rouge; Washington University, St. Louis;
Dallas Museum of Art; Pontevedre Spain; Cornell
University; and Portland Museum of Art

2001

Architectural Record Houses Award for Tubac Residence
AIA Arizona Honor Awards for Tubac House and 400
Rubio Avenue Studio
Member of PA Awards Jury and LA/AIA California Awards
Jury
Visiting Critic at Massachusetts Institute of Technology
and Washington University, St. Louis
Lectures: University of Michigan; University of Arkansas;
San Diego Museum of Contemporary Art; Texas
Technical University; University of Texas at Houston;

San Juan Capistrano Museum of Architecture;
Virginia Technical University; Massachusetts Institute
of Technology; University of California at Berkeley;
University at Buffalo; Arizona State University; and
University of Michigan
Exhibited work at GA Gallery

2000

AR+D Emerging Architecture Award
The Architectural League of New York Emerging Voices
Award
I. D. Magazine Annual Design Award for Rubio Avenue
Studio
AIA Central Arizona Home of the Year for Catalina House
Exhibition: *Ten Shades of Green* at the Architectural
League of New York
Visiting Professor at Harvard Graduate School of Design
and University of Arizona
Visiting Critic at Yale University
Lectures: University of Minnesota; Taliesin West;
University of Arizona; the Architectural League of
New York; AIA Las Vegas; University of Virginia;
Harvard University; and University of Texas at Austin
Exhibited work at GA Gallery

1999

Lectures: Auburn University and Rural Studio
Exhibited work at GA Gallery

1997–1998

Architectural Record House Award for Convent
Avenue Studios
I. D. Magazine Annual Design Award for Convent
Avenue Studios
Roy P. Drachman Award for Convent Avenue Studios
Founding Board of Directors Member of Civitas Sonoran,
the Environmental Design Council of Tucson
Lectures: University of Arizona and University of
New Mexico

1993–1996

Licensed to practice in Arizona and launched
Rick Joy Architect, Ltd.
Progressive Architecture Young Architects Award
Arizona Home of the Year for Joy/Millen Residence
The Architectural League of New York Young
Architects Award
Second son, Eli, born
Lecture at Arizona State University

1990–1993

Received Bachelor of Architecture degree from
University of Arizona
First son, Ethan, born
Worked in the offices of William P. Bruder Architect on
the project team of the Phoenix Central Library
Designed and built own family house in Tucson

1985–1990

Moved to Tucson
Studied architecture at the University of Arizona

1976–1984

Studied music at the University of Maine and performed
as a symphony percussionist
Performed as a drummer in various venues on the
East Coast
Married Jean Millen
Worked part-time as a carpenter
Studied color theory, sculpture, and photography
at the Portland School of Art

1958

Born in Dover-Foxcroft, Maine, on December 25
Lived in Ipswich, Massachusetts, until age twelve
Attended high school in Old Town, Maine

Office Associates

Current Associates

Amal Anoohi
Daniel Badillo
Carla Chang Mata
Felipe Combeau
Liane Ee
Eva Hagberg Fisher
Miguel Gonzalez
Natalia Zieman Hayes
Erik Johnson
Annheliza Jordaan
Rick Joy
Claudia Kappl
Joshua Kievenaar
Kurt Krueger
Silvia Lucchetta
Matt Luck
Dan Martin
Christopher Pela
Alan Purvis

Tofan Rafati
Celia Ramirez
Gustavo Ramirez
Colby Ritter
Alyssa Sackman
Jaime Pages Sanchez
Bach Tran
Jay Williams
Nancy Wilson
Marybel Rodriguez
    Zepeda

Former Associates

Jason Argyropoulos
Gabriele Balconi
James Barnfield
Matthew Bishop
Colin Bruce
Franz Buhler
Kevin Burson
Alice Carin
Howard Chu
Chad Cornet
Hubert d'Autremont
Holly Damerell
Anthony DiMari
Patrick Doty
Luat Duong
Michael Elliot
Curtis Eppley
Jack Eure
Chris Ford
Jared Fulton
Louise Girling
Madeline Gradillas
Chelsea Grassinger
Stephanie Griffith
Mohamad Hafez
Kathy Hancox

Dave Hardin
David Harrill
Michael Hasey
Cade Hayes
Darci Hazelbaker
Nicole Herd
Ben Holland
Paco Francisco Izquierdo
Tyler Jorgenson
Eli Joy
Ethan Joy
Jacob Kalinowski
Dylan King
Eleni Koryzi
Carl Koski
Michael Kothke
Kimberley Largey
Malcom Lee
Jennifer Little
Daniela Lopez
Oscar Lopez
Sarah Dickerson Luck
Heiman Luk
Will MacIvor
Minette Martin
Lisa Martinez

Caryn McCarthy
David McGregor
Ian McGregor
Matthew Miller
Mark Mismash
Ruth Mitchell
Anna Moelk
Philipp Neher
Evo Nellison
Nicolas Norero
Jerry Park
Rob Paulus
Kathleen Paxton
Shawn Protz
Michael Reinauld
Jesus Edmundo Robles
Patrick Ruggiero Jr.
Dale Rush
Jane Schmitt-Ibarra
Amanda Schwarz
Michael
    Schwindenhammer
Fergus Scott
Scott Semple
Maartje Steenkamp
Suzanne Stefan

Kevin Stewart
David Thomas
Andy Tinucci
Nina Tinucci
Daniel Toole
Quang Truong
Klara Valent
Nichio Vallian
Paula Versalovic
Bruno Vidal
Sarah Wellesley
Michael Whitchurch
Michaelle Williams
Kami Witherspoon
Scott Woodward
Andres Zegers
Matias Zegers
Huopu Zhang

Project Credits

ADOBE CANYON HOUSE
Patagonia, Arizona
DESIGN: 2003
CONSTRUCTION: 2003–2005
HOUSE: 1,370 square feet
TERRACE: 780 square feet
PROJECT TEAM: Rick Joy, Cade Hayes,
Mark Mishmash, Juliet Spertus, Verginie Stanley
BUILDER: Rick Joy Architects

DESERT NOMAD HOUSE
Tucson, Arizona
DESIGN: 1999
CONSTRUCTION: 2001–2002, 2005–2006
HOUSE: 1,540 square feet
PROJECT TEAM: Rick Joy, Andy Tinucci, Cade Hayes,
Chelsea Grassinger, Franz Buhler
CONSULTANTS: Southwest Structural Engineers,
Otterbein Mechanical Engineering
BUILDER: Rick Joy Architects

VENTANA CANYON RESIDENCE
Tucson, Arizona
DESIGN: 2004
CONSTRUCTION: 2004–2008
RESIDENCE: 6,780 square feet
TERRACE: 2,570 square feet
PROJECT TEAM: Rick Joy, Michael Kothke,
Cade Hayes, Kathy Hancox, Madeline Gradillas,
Dale Rush, Chris Ford, Claudia Valent, Juliet Spertus,
Verginie Stanley
CONSULTANTS: Harris Structural Engineering
BUILDER: W. J. Lang Construction

NAPA TREE HOUSE
Napa County, California
DESIGN: 2004
CONSTRUCTION: 2005–2006
HOUSE: 4,450 square feet
TERRACE: 1,870 square feet
PROJECT TEAM: Rick Joy, Kathy Hancox, Cade Hayes,
Michael Kothke
CONSULTANTS: Harris Structural Engineering, Sterk
Engineering
BUILDER: Grassi & Associates

WOODSTOCK VERMONT FARM
Woodstock, Vermont
DESIGN: 2007
CONSTRUCTION: 2007–2008
HOUSE: 3,890 square feet
Barn: 5,410 square feet
TERRACE: 1,750 square feet
PROJECT TEAM: Rick Joy, Dale Rush, Philipp Neher,
Nicolas Norero, Madeline Gradillas, Claudia Valent,
James Barnfield, Hubert d'Autremont, Louise Girling
CONSULTANTS: Harris Structural Engineering,
Michael Boucher Landscape Architects,
Ljusarkitektur P+O AB
BUILDER: Colby & Tobiason

AMANGIRI
Kane County, Utah
DESIGN: 1999–2006
CONSTRUCTION: 2006–2008
RESORT: 86,960 square feet
TERRACES AND POOLS: 81,890 square feet
PROJECT TEAM: I-10 Studio: Rick Joy,
Marwan Al-Sayed, Wendell Burnette, Colin Bruce,
Joby Dutton, Arlee Fisher, Madeline Gradillas,
Cade Hayes, Michael Kothke, Patrick Magness,
Philipp Neher, Neil Patel, Michael Powell,
Jena Rimkus, Scott Roeder, Dale Rush,
Scott Scales, Suzanne Stefan, Brianna Tovsen,
Matthew Trzebiatowski, Claudia Valent
CONSULTANTS: Harris Structural Engineering,
Woodward Engineering, Kunka Engineering,
Stantec Consulting, Ljusarkitektur P&O AB,
Michael Boucher Landscape Architecture,
Wardin Cockriel Associates, Tait Solar, Aqua Design
International, Construction Consultants
BUILDER: Oakland Construction Company

LONE MOUNTAIN RANCH HOUSE
Golden, New Mexico
DESIGN: 2009
CONSTRUCTION: 2010–2012
HOUSE: 7,770 square feet
TERRACE: 960 square feet
PROJECT TEAM: Rick Joy, Philipp Neher,
Nicolas Norero, Luat Duong, Stephanie Griffith,
Claudia Kappl, Daniela Lopez, Jerry Park
CONSULTANTS: Harris Structural Engineering,
Dennis Engineering Company
BUILDER: Kenderdine Construction

SUN VALLEY HOUSE
Sun Valley, Idaho
DESIGN: 2010–2011
CONSTRUCTION: 2011–2013
HOUSE: 7,900 square feet
TERRACE: 1,080 square feet
PROJECT TEAM: Rick Joy, Matt Luck, Howard Chu,
Natalia Zieman Hayes, Claudia Kappl, Luat Duong,
Bruno Vidal, Stephanie Griffith, Patrick Ruggiero,
Eleni Koryzi, Sarah Dickerson Luck
CONSULTANTS: Harris Structural Engineering,
Michael Boucher Landscape Architects, CLL Concept
Lighting Lab LLC, Benchmark Associates
BUILDER: Schuchart/Dow

NEW YORK LOFT
New York, New York
DESIGN: 2011
CONSTRUCTION: 2012
LOFT: 940 square feet
PROJECT TEAM: Rick Joy, Claudia Kappl
BUILDER: Matt Galvin Builders

LE CABANON
Turks and Caicos Islands
DESIGN: 2013
CONSTRUCTION: 2014–2016
HOUSE: 3,150 square feet
TERRACE: 2,620 square feet
PROJECT TEAM: Rick Joy, Gustavo Ramirez,
Claudia Kappl, Matthew Bishop, Matt Luck,
Philipp Neher, Steve Martin, Natalia Zieman Hayes,
Shawn Protz, James Hamilton Architects
CONSULTANTS: Harris Structural Engineering,
CLL Concept Lighting Lab LLC, Barbara Underwood
Landscaping, Reg Hough Associates, David Soares
BUILDER: Norstar Group

TENNYSON 205

Mexico City, Mexico

DESIGN: 2013–2015

CONSTRUCTION: 2015–2018

BUILDING: 10,920 square feet

TERRACE: 1,990 square feet

PROJECT TEAM: Rick Joy, Philipp Neher,
Natalia Zieman Hayes, Christopher Pela,
Marybel Rodriguez, Suzanne Stefan, Heiman Luk,
FRB Arquitectectos Asociados

CONSULTANTS: CLL Concept Lighting Lab LLC,
Entorno Taller de Paisaje, Rodolfo Padilla, IESH
Instalaciones, Jorge Walls

BUILDER: P&G (Rodolfo Padilla and Gilberto Gómez)

BAYHOUSE

DESIGN: 2015

CONSTRUCTION: 2016–2018

HOUSE: 6,980 square feet

PROJECT TEAM: Rick Joy, Matt Luck, Natalia Zieman
Hayes, Bach Tran, Oscar Lopez

CONSULTANTS: Silman Engineering, Altieri Sebor
Wieber, Michael Boucher Landscape Architects,
CLL Concept Lighting Lab LLC, Simpson Gumpertz
& Heger, Daniel Falasco Consulting Engineers, Bellport
Design, Cramer Consulting

BUILDER: Schuchart Dow

**PRINCETON TRANSIT HALL
AND MARKET**

Princeton, New Jersey

DESIGN: 2012–2013

CONSTRUCTION: 2014–2018

STATION: 2,240 square feet

STORE: 8,330 square feet

STORE, EXTERIOR LOADING: 330 square feet

CANOPY: 2,840 square feet

BIKE STORAGE: 1,050 square feet

LOT 7 BIKE STORAGE: 370 square feet

PROJECT TEAM: Rick Joy, Matt Luck, Natalia Zieman
Hayes, Bach Tran, Shawn Protz, Philipp Neher,
Luat Duong, Heiman Luk

CONSULTANTS: Arup Engineering, R.W. Sullivan
Engineering, Roofmeadow, Two Twelve Associates,
Construction Specifications, Davis Langdon,
Simpson Gumpertz and Heger, CLL Concept
Lighting Lab LLC

COLLABORATORS: Beyer Blinder Bell Planners,
Michael Van Valkenburgh and Associates,
Vanasse Hangen Brustlin, Affiliated Engineers, Inc.,
Tillett Lighting Design, BFJ Planning, Nitsch
Engineering, Craul Land Scientists, WC3 Design

BUILDER: Turner Construction Company